THE
EDGES

Poetry & Prose

CARO HENRY

KemoDog Press
BALTIMORE, MARYLAND
kemodogpress.com

Library of Congress Control Number: 2024918401

Printed in the United States of America.
Imprint: KemoDog Press

Names: Henry, Caro, author.
Title: The edges / Caro Henry.
Description: Baltimore, MD: KemoDog Press, 2024.
Identifiers: LCCN: 2024918401 | ISBN: 979-8-9914912-1-1 (hardcover) | 979-8-218-49156-7 (paperback) | 979-8-9914912-0-4 (ebook)
Subjects: LCSH American poetry--21st century. | Nature--Poetry. | War--Poetry. | Love--Poetry. | Time--Poetry. | BISAC POETRY / Subjects & Themes / General | POETRY / Subjects & Themes / Animals & Nature | POETRY / Caribbean & Latin American | POETRY / Subjects & Themes / Death, Grief, Loss | POETRY / Subjects & Themes / Political & Protest | POETRY / Subjects & Themes / War
Classification: LCC PS3608 .E67 E 2024 | DDC 811.6--dc23

Cover design by Laura Simon
Cover art photo by Caro Henry

First Edition: September 2024

For my husband and daughter

TABLE OF CONTENTS

INTRODUCTION

I am fascinated with the liminal. I mean the edges and borders that provide a transition from one state of existence to another.

Within liminal spaces, doors open to surprises, portals transport, and nature reveals its transformative power. These spaces encourage us to venture into the extraordinary, embrace the unfamiliar, and uncover the marvels that exist beyond our awareness.

In this anthology of poetry and prose, I explore the edges, those liminal spaces. At times, I inhabit them and venture into past, present, future, and otherworldly realms.

My aim is to touch you with my words and evoke deep emotions within you.

Divided into six sections, each segment of this anthology is a portal to a different realm.

Love & War: A celebration of love in all its forms and complexities and an exploration of human suffering in the raw and brutal realities of war.

Nature & Cosmos: A journey through the untamed wilderness and boundless expanse of the universe, where the mysteries of existence unravel in whispers of wind and starlight.

Time & Memories: Threads of reminiscence woven into time's fabric, where nostalgia and reflection entwine.

Seasons & Liminal Spaces: Capturing time's ebb and flow in seasons and liminal spaces, between what was, what is, and what will be.

Observations & Views: Perspectives painted with the strokes of keen observation and introspection, offering glimpses into the diverse landscapes of the human mind.

Wounds & Contemplations: A canvas of healing and introspection, where individuals wear scars as badges of resilience and contemplations resound in the chambers of the soul.

Each piece is a reflection, each section a journey. This anthology testifies to the power of words in illuminating the beauty and complexity of the human experience.

I hope my writings inspire, challenge, and transform you, just like they do me.

LOVE & WAR

You cannot find peace by avoiding life.
—VIRGINIA WOOLF

LOVE

COME AWAY

Come away with me, and be my love,
Let's explore the vast unknown,
As we sail the seven seas,
Discover treasures not yet shown.

Together we'll visit ancient lands,
And marvel at modern sights,
From mountains reaching for the sky,
To peaceful meadows, bathed in light.

Come away with me, and be my love,
On wings of dreams, we'll fly,
Across the zones, we'll journey far,
Reconnect with friends gone by.

We'll share stories of our lives,
Cherish moments, big and small,
Savoring scones and laughter,
Creating memories to recall.

Come away with me, and be my love,
Down winding roads we'll roam,
Embracing nature's wondrous gifts,
Flora and fauna, we'll call home.

In this world, we'll travel hand in hand,
Facing challenges, side by side,
Conquering all life throws our way,
Our love, unbreakable, our guide.

So, come away with me, and be my love,
Let's embark on this grand endeavor,
Together we'll navigate this world,
Our hearts entwined, forever and ever.

EROS

It was night again and as
I felt for your presence in

Darkness not yet complete,
Yawning stillness forced me to

Consider the warm contemplation
Seen earlier in your eyes.

Calculated to a degree to hasten
To a fever pitch; to feel slowly,

Then hear the rushing moon
Breathing across a light-riddled sky.

Cutting slivers of fleshy passion;
Forcing raw explanations again,

As the room rolls majestically,
Musically, in its own rhythmic

Order of life; reborn, renewed,
And life gathers us in closer,

To face yet again the truths we
Try to hide in pale sunlight.

FUGUE IN BLUE

I hear the music
    And as our souls
        Twirl, spin, negotiate
           Each turn
I saw them dance
    Their figures
        Blurred blue
           Loving, swirling,
Sometimes fused

Ah! the longing
    Do souls ache?
        Pillowed sweetly in
           Repose, feebly laid

As the lute whines
    The nascent dawn
        Clasps us to her breast
        Then, I awaken
Feel the weight
Of you there,
Hear your
Sleep-stained breaths

MOTHER'S LOVE

I am a mother.
> My love flame burns bright;
> The words I speak, the tone I use
> Light her path, her journey through life.

I am a mother.
> From nascent flutters of thought,
> To the moment I first held her,
> I swore to protect and nurture.

I am a mother.
> Through sleepless nights, weary days,
> Sacrificed my own wants, own desires,
> Ensured her happiness, fulfilled her needs.

I am a mother.
> In her teen years of angst and yearnings,
> Supportive when emotions heightened,
> Attentive when winds of change blew fiercely.

I am a mother.
> Torn between desire to protect, need to let go,
> Reaffirmed her worth, her potential,
> Encouraged her to embrace her dreams, to fly.

I am a mother.
> There, as she emerged from her chrysalis of adolescence;
> There, as she learned to navigate the complexities of
> adulthood;
> There, as she transformed into a successful adult.

I am a mother.
   My love knows no bounds;
   It is an unbreakable bond,
   Transcending time and space.

Because I am a mother—
   My love flame burns bright;
   The words I speak, the tone I use,
   Light her path, her journey through life.

SENSUAL

Your gentle yet electric touch
Igniting a fire within me
Each caress causing me to
Unravel
Lips soft and hungry
Meet in a dance of
Desire and surrender

Skin against skin
Rubbing teasing
A symphony of
Longing and pleasure

Your voice breathing
Caressing my skin
Surrender complete
As my inhibitions fade
And a hunger awakens

Every kiss every touch
A thousand tiny explosions
Scattering my essence into
A million little pieces

Hands exploring every curve
Every angle
Lips tracing a path of fire
That leaves me trembling

Kisses on my neck

My collarbone
My every inch of exposed skin
And I feel myself teetering
On the edge of a precipice
Ready to fall into the
Abyss of ecstasy

Ecstasy that easily
Shatters me into pieces
Then rebuilds me as new
That leaves me breathless
Wanting more

WHY IS IT?

Why is it so hard
To find words
That pour, stream,
Flow, wine-like;

That slide, glide,
Slip gradually,
Unobtrusively?
Why is it so hard

For my bruised heart
To say
I love you,
I need you?

When my salve
Exists in your arms,
Entangled
In your lips.

WAR

BATTLE SCARS

The hands of war tighten their grip,
A symphony of horror with malevolent notes.
Battlefields, once vibrant with life,
Now wear cloaks of destruction.
The air, heavy with the acrid stench of
Ammo and fear, spins
Tales of anguish and despair.
Death, its appetite insatiable,
Devours souls, their cries echo,
Lost in the cacophony.

Amidst the fray, hearts shatter,
As the cruel hand of fate reaches out
Separating loved ones.
A mother, eyes brimming
With unshed tears,
Clutches the tattered
Photograph of her son.
Memories dance in her mind as she
Traces the contours of his face,
Fingers trembling.

In a foreign land, a man,
Displaced and uprooted,
Clings to remnants of
His shattered homeland.
A foreign language and
Unfamiliar faces replace
Familiar sights and sounds.
He longs for the scent of

His native soil, the embrace of
Loved ones, the comfort of belonging.

War horrors paint
Vivid canvasses of desolation.
The earth, scarred and ravaged,
Bear the marks of countless battles;
Once-lush fields transform
Into desolate wastelands.
Trees, barren of leaves,
Stand like sentinels of despair,
Branches twisted, reaching
For a touch of life.

Oh, the horror of war!
That master of cruelty,
Tears families asunder,
Leaves trails of broken hearts,
Shattered dreams.
So, humanity weeps,
Its soul shattered,
As sorrow and guilt
Embrace each
Survivor's heart.

CONSEQUENTLY

Consequently, nations clash like thunder and lightning,
Their differences sparking fires that engulf the land,
As power-hungry leaders, thirsty for dominance,
Fuel the flames of conflict with their rhetoric.

Consequently, borders become battlefields,
Where soldiers march to the beat of war drums,
And families are torn apart, hearts heavy with sorrow,
As they flee from the devastation of their homes.

Consequently, the innocent suffers the most,
Caught in the crossfire of political ambition,
Their lives shattered like fragile glass,
Dreams crushed under the weight of war.

Consequently, the world watches in horror,
As nations wage wars of aggression,
Their reasons obscured by propaganda,
Their true motives hidden beneath a veil of lies.

Consequently, hatred spreads like a virus,
Infecting hearts and minds with prejudice and fear,
Tearing apart the fabric of humanity,
Leaving behind scars that may never heal.

Consequently, generations bear the burden,
Of the sins of their ancestors,
Haunted by memories of conflict,
As they struggle to build a world free from strife.

Consequently, peace becomes a distant dream,
A flickering flame in the darkness of chaos,
But hope lingers in the hearts of the resilient,
Who refuse to let war define their existence.

Consequently, we must strive for understanding,
To bridge the divides that separate us,
Find common ground amidst the turmoil,
And build a future where peace can prevail.

Consequently, empathy must be the language we speak,
With understanding a bridge of connection,
Compassion an armor against the flames of hatred,
Love a beacon of hope in times of despair.

Consequently, dialogue should be our weapon of choice,
Our words instruments of peace,
With listening superseding the roar of cannons,
Negotiation paving the path to resolution.

Consequently, let education be our shield,
Let knowledge dispel the shadows of ignorance,
Empowering minds reject the call to violence,
And nurturing hearts embrace harmony.

Consequently, let us rewrite the narrative of war,
Where conflicts are resolved through diplomacy,
Where justice triumphs over vengeance,
Where wounds of the past find healing in forgiveness.

HISTORY LESSON

War, a relentless specter, weaves its tale of woe;
A symphony of horrors, echoing through time,
From the trenches of World War I's desolation,
To the blood-stained fields of World War II's agony.

In the trenches, where the earth swallowed hope,
Soldiers stood as pawns in a deadly game,
Gasping for air through the choking fumes,
Their bodies bearing scars of a mechanized slaughter.
Mud-caked boots and weary souls,
Marching toward the abyss of human folly.

World War II, a canvas painted in shades of despair,
The Holocaust's chilling embrace,
A darkness that engulfed six million souls,
Leaving behind a void that can never be filled.
Cities ablaze, skies torn asunder,
As the world witnessed the depths of inhumanity.

And in the present, the echoes of past sorrows,
Russia and Ukraine locked in a dance of death,
Bearing witness to lives torn asunder,
In the name of power and pride.
Israel and Palestine, a tale of ancient wounds,
Bleeding afresh in a land steeped in strife.

The cries of the innocent, a haunting refrain,
Among the rubble of shattered dreams,
Children of war, born into a world of chaos,
Their laughter drowned by the thunder of cannons.

The scars of conflict, etched deep in the earth,
A reminder of the price we pay for our folly.

Still, in the darkness, a flicker of hope,
A yearning for peace, a plea for understanding.
In the midst of chaos, the human spirit shines,
Resilient, defiant in the face of despair.
May we heed the lessons of the past,
And strive for a future where war's horrors are but a
memory.

HOPE

Amidst thundering explosions and shattered dreams,
The cries of anguish and rivers of tears,
There blooms a fragile hope, like a delicate flower,
Pushing through the cracked earth, seeking the light.

It is the whisper of a lily, soft and serene,
Unfolding its petals in defiance of chaos,
Each blossom a prayer, each petal a plea,
For peace to reign, for harmony to prevail.

And as the soldiers lay down their arms,
Their battle-weary bodies yearning for respite,
Their voices rise in unison, a symphony of hope,
Echoing through the war-torn valleys.

Soon, the sun emerges from behind the clouds,
Casting its golden rays upon scarred landscapes,
It paints a tapestry of peace, where shadows recede,
And wounds begin to heal, slowly but surely.

In the heart of war, in the darkest night,
Hope flickers, a flame that refuses to be extinguished,
It dances with resilience, igniting the spirit,
Guiding us toward a future bathed in tranquility.

For even in the middle of chaos and strife,
The longing for peace echoes in every soul,
And though the path may be treacherous and long,
Hope, like a beacon, leads us home.

IDEOLOGICAL WAR

Where echoes of dissent
Ripple through the fabric of a nation's soul,
A war of ideologies unfolds, fierce and unyielding.

On one side, shadows whisper of authoritarian allure,
A siren song of order in a world untamed,
Where fear breeds the desire for a firm hand,
To quell the storms of uncertainty,
To silence the cries for freedom's dance.

Opposing them, a chorus rises, voices of defiance,
Champions of democracy's sacred flame,
Carrying the legacy of founding fathers' dreams,
In the beating heart of liberty's embrace.

The battleground stretches beyond mere mortal realms,
Into the very essence of belief and conviction,
A clash of wills, a collision of truths,
Where the air crackles with tension,
And the ground trembles with the weight of choice.

Families torn asunder, friendships severed,
As lines are drawn in the sand of principle,
And loyalty wavers in the face of conviction.

Wait! A flicker of hope in the chaos,
A beacon of light in the darkness,
Hands clasped in solidarity, voices raised in unity,
Attesting to the resilience of a people unbowed.

The ghosts of patriots past watch with solemn gaze,
Their spirits woven into the tapestry of the present,
Their legacy a guiding light in the storm,
A reminder of the price of freedom, the cost of apathy.

As the war rages on, uncertainty hangs heavy in the air,
A veil of doubt draped over the horizon,
But in the hearts of the people, a fire burns bright,
A flame of defiance, a spark of strength.

For the fight for democracy is not just a battle,
But a hymn of defiance, a symphony of unity,
A pledge to uphold the sacred trust,
And in the clash of swords and ideals,
The true measure of a nation's strength is revealed,
Not in its power, but in its people.

SACRIFICIAL

On the outskirts of a city,
Where chaos and destruction reigned,
A van laden with sustenance and hope,
Navigates through the labyrinth of destruction.

World Central Kitchen volunteers,
Bearers of compassion in a land besieged,
Their mission clear, their spirits resolute,
To feed the hungry, to soothe the weary soul.

The sun, a silent witness to their journey,
Paints the sky with hues of longing and sorrow,
As they traverse the scarred streets,
Echoes of suffering reverberating in their wake.

Buildings, once proud monuments of life,
Now stand as silent specimens of devastation,
Their hollow shells whispering tales of loss,
Of lives upturned by the cruel hand of war.

And in a moment, swift and merciless,
Rockets rain down from the heavens,
Shattering the fragile peace of the day,
Tearing through the van.

Smoke and sorrow intertwine in the air,
As the van becomes a tomb of shattered dreams,
Innocent lives snuffed out in a heartbeat,
Their sacrifice a symphony of tragedy.

The world weeps for the fallen souls,
Whose only crime was empathy, whose only sin was
kindness,
Their memory etched in the annals of war,
A stark reminder of the human cost of conflict.

So, among the ashes and pain,
Their legacy lives on, a flickering flame of hope,
A testament to the enduring power of love,
In a world scarred by violence and strife.

As the sun dips below the horizon,
Casting a golden glow over the ravaged landscape,
We hope for an end to this strife, remembering
Their spirits linger like gentle whispers in the wind.

WAR HAUNTINGS

In the war's crucible,
They became like brittle leaves tossed by a relentless wind,
Their spirits flitting across the desolate landscape.

Blood-soaked fields bore witness to their sacrifice,
As life's flame flickered and faded.

And in the end,
Only the ghosts of valor remained,
Haunting the hearts of the living.

NATURE & COSMOS

Look deep into nature, and then you will understand everything better.

—ALBERT EINSTEIN

NATURE

CROWS DESCENDING

Crows descending in the backyard,
A symphony of black wings beating,
A cacophony of caws, a chorus of beaks clicking,
Drawn by food in bird feeders, a feast laid out.

The crows glide from branch to branch,
Their eyes bright, their feathers sleek,
Perching on the house's gutters, claws scrabbling,
They survey the scene.

Two cats watch from a distance, eyes narrowed, tails
twitching;
The crows pay them no mind, their attention on the prize—
The feast before them, a bounty of seeds,
Mixed nut meats and suet.

The cats tense, ready to pounce, but they know better;
These crows demand respect with their garish ways,
Plus, they are too many;
The crows know this too; they are not afraid.

Their confidence evident in the way they descend,
The way they move and eat;
As the sun begins to set, the crows take flight,
Cawing their goodbyes;

Their bellies full, happy, content;
The cats watch them go, their eyes following as
The crows disappear into the horizon,
Shadows against the sky.

FOG WATCHING

I.
The morning sun peeks through the frosty air,
As tendrils of fog creep on silent feet,
Enveloping the world with hushed despair,
A winter shroud, a mystical white sheet.

The trees stand tall, adorned in icy lace,
Their branches engraved with delicate frost,
Like whispers of winter, frozen embrace,
Nature's artwork, beautifully embossed.

And there, amidst the fog's ethereal haze,
A bright orange fox emerges, swift and sly,
Disguised by the mist's mysterious ways,
In search of sustenance, its keen eyes spy.

Oh, winter morning, so serene and cold,
With fog and frost, a beauty to behold.

II.
As dawn breaks, the fog begins to retreat,
Unveiling the world, slowly bit by bit,
Revealing the wonders beneath its sheet,
The evergreens, adorned in emerald knit.

The frost on leaves, adorns in lacy lines,
Bejeweled ice crystals, shimmering with grace,
The evidence of nature's grand design,
A frozen canvas, woven with no haste.

The bright orange fox, in stealth it does roam,
Its paws treading lightly on frozen ground,
A predator's instinct, its senses honed,
Hunting for prey, without making a sound.

Oh, winter morning, with fog and frost laced,
A magical world, by nature embraced.

III.
The fog has vanished, a memory now,
Replaced by the warmth of the rising sun,
Yet the frost's touch still clings to each branch, bough,
A reminder of what the cold has done.

The evergreen leaves, resilient and strong,
Stand proud and tall, amidst the winter's chill,
Symbols of endurance, all season long,
Guardians of the forest, steadfast and still.

The bright orange fox, with its fiery hue,
Now blends with the vibrant colors of day,
Its hunting complete, its purpose now through,
It vanishes, into the woods to stay.

Oh, winter morning, with fog and frost gone,
Leaving behind a world, pristine and drawn.

IV.
As the day progresses, the fog's hold fades,
Yet, in my mind, its presence still lingers,
The ethereal beauty that it conveyed,
In every thought, extending its fingers.

The frost's touch, like a kind lover's caress,
Has left its mark on nature's every face,
Attesting to winter's cold finesse,

A reminder of its temporary embrace.

And the bright orange fox, forever free,
Roams through the woods, a creature of the wild,
A symbol of resilience, what could be,
In a world where nature is reconciled.

Oh, winter morning, with fog and frost passed,
A timeless beauty, forever to last.

AN ODE TO GREEN

From towering trees, with their majestic presence,
To the blades of grass gently caressed by my hand,
You bring forth a world of serene beauty,
A sanctuary of calm and tranquility.

Green, you adorn the Earth,
Painting, decorating in emerald shades,
With each nuanced hue, a narrative unfurls,
A tale of adaptations, mysterious revelations.

The cacti, armed with their formidable spines,
Endure in deserts, where water is scarce,
Their succulent bodies, reservoirs of vitality,
In arid lands, where resilience flourishes.

Within rainforests, your domain thrives,
A symphony of green, where life finds sustenance,
Leaves in countless hues, forming a lush canopy,
A sanctuary for creatures, untamed and free.

The chameleon, a master of camouflage,
Merges effortlessly, unnoticed by curious gazes,
With stealth and elegance, it navigates the trees,
Invisible amidst the verdant tapestry.

The tree frog, agile and nimble,
Jumps from leaf to leaf, where it rests,
Its skin, adorned in shades of lime,
A vibrant mantle, a tribute to nature's artistry.

And in the depths of the vast ocean,
Green prevails, in hues both vivid and pure,
Seaweeds and algae, forming an underwater forest,
A haven for creatures, a vibrant realm of life.

Green, you embody the embrace of life,
A color that sustains, pervading every space,
In fields and forests, in the depths of oceans,
I shall forever cherish your timeless beauty.

Allow me to offer my hymn to you, oh green,
In prose that flows, a melody yet unheard,
For you embody the divine essence of our Earth,
A glorious celebration of life's immeasurable worth.

NATURE, RED

A hawk soared with grace high above in the sky, where the heavens touch the earth. Its wings, an elegant display of power, carried it effortlessly through the boundless azure expanse. With each beat, the wind whispered sweet melodies, as if nature itself acknowledged the majesty of this predator.

Down below, nestled among the verdant canopy, a plump dove, innocent and unsuspecting, danced among the trees. Its soft coos echoed through the woods, a lullaby that embraced the tranquility of the forest. Oblivious to the imminent danger that loomed above, the dove reveled in the serenity of its surroundings.

But the hawk, a predator born to hunt, had honed its instincts to perfection. Its keen eyes locked onto the plump dove, a jewel amidst the emerald foliage. The raptor's descent, swift and silent, cut through the air like a blade, casting an ominous shadow upon the peaceful scene below.

In a heartbeat, the world shattered. The raptor's talons, with razor-like precision, gripped the dove mercilessly. Its beak, a curved weapon of destruction, descended upon the innocent prey. Feathers scattered like leaves caught in a tempest, floating aimlessly in the wake of chaos.

The plump dove, once full of life and vitality, now lay still in the clutches of the hawk. Its delicate form, once a symbol of peace, now an offering to the unforgiving laws of nature.

The silence that followed was profound, a mournful requiem for a life lost.

And so, I came upon the angelic feathers on one of my walks and imagined the brutal act, as the hawk tore into the flesh of its prize. I mourned the life lost, even as I recognized the continuing circle of life, an eternal cycle of beauty and brutality, forever etched in the annals of the natural world.

OCEAN VIEW

In hushed stillness,
Night's hold slackens;

Dawn's gilding, gently born,
Tiptoes on the ocean;

Reflecting off the waves,
Its creamsicle colors;

Bathing the world
In warm, ethereal bliss.

ON GOLDEN POND

A fiery dawn consumes
The pond where lilies wade;
Their green leaves glistening,
Bathed in the morning's grace.

Gold-tinged rays shine
With a divine brilliance,
As light breezes caress,
And birds sing their greeting.

RIVERSIDE

A golden cascade
Paints the sky
With hues of fire

A symphony of colors
Mirrored in the silky
Ribbon of the river

Where the box turtles
Climb on partially submerged
Rocks and branches

In the embrace of morning's desire

WOODLAND MUSINGS

When I am among the trees,
I am in a sacred place,
A place where I can escape,
Where the world's chaos recedes.
Every step I take,
Every rustle beneath my feet
Brings me to a closer connection
With the earth.

When I am among the trees,
Leaves softly swish in diffused light,
Birds speak in their language of melodies,
And the wind's whisper cools my skin.
The fragrant air, infused with the
Scent of moss, damp soil, and
Fecund leaves, becomes my incense,
Rejuvenating my spirit.

When I am among the trees,
I sense a kinship with their collective,
The interconnected roots that anchor them,
Branches that reach to touch the heavens.
I am reminded of my own roots,
My own connection to this world;
Reminded of the importance of being present,
Of embracing the beauty that surrounds me.

When I am among the trees,
I am on a spiritual journey,
A chance to reconnect with myself

And with something greater.
In the stillness of the woods,
I find clarity and peace as
Worries and stresses fade away,
Replaced by awe and gratitude.

WOODS IN THE MIST

In the stillness of dawn, the mist seems to blanket the world in winding sheets. The trees stand like ghostly sentinels, their outlines blurred by the swirling fog.

I walk along the path, the crunch of leaves beneath my feet muffled by the thick, damp air.

The mist clings to my skin, cool and clammy, as I make my way through the woods. It is a morning for introspection, for quiet contemplation.

The world feels muted, muffled, as though the fog has deadened all sound and sensation.

As I walk deeper into the woods, the fog grows thicker still.

It is like walking through a dream, where everything is vague and indistinct. The path ahead is barely visible, and I move slowly, feeling my way through the mist.

Still, there is a beauty to the fog, a haunting quality that resonates within me. The mist transforms the woods into a place of mystery and magic, where anything is possible.

And so I walk, lost in my thoughts and the swirling mist. I feel as though I am wandering through fantasyland, where the impossible is made real.

As the sun rises higher in the sky, the mist begins to lift, the world becoming more focused, more defined.

And I emerge from the woods, feeling refreshed, renewed.

The fog has lifted, but the memory of that misty morning lingers.

COSMOS

APOPHIS

In the vast expanse of the celestial tapestry, where the stars paint a cosmic masterpiece, there exists a celestial wanderer known as Apophis.

A tempestuous embodiment of darkness and mystery, Apophis weaves its way through the depths of the cosmos, an enigma that leaves astronomers and stargazers in awe.

Born from the primordial chaos, Apophis is a serpent of the night sky, slithering through the astral realms with a grace that belies its fearsome reputation. Its serpentine form, adorned with scales that shimmer like onyx in the twilight, is a testament to its power and ancient lineage.

Apophis, named after the Egyptian god of chaos and destruction, commands a gravitational force that can shift the balance of celestial bodies. Its presence is a reminder of the delicate equilibrium that governs the universe, a constant reminder that chaos is an ever-present force, lurking in the darkness.

The astronomers watch in anticipation as Apophis approaches, its path intersecting with Earth's orbit.

Fear and curiosity dance hand in hand, for this celestial dance has the potential to alter the course of our existence. The enigmatic wanderer becomes a symbol of uncertainty, reminding us of the fragility of our mortal existence.

A sense of wonder blooms amidst the fear. Apophis, with its dark beauty, captivates the imagination.

It is a symbol of the unknown, a reminder that there are realms beyond our comprehension, waiting to be explored.

Like a cosmic riddle, Apophis beckons us to delve deeper into the mysteries of the universe, to seek understanding in the face of the unknown.

As Apophis fades into the cosmic abyss, leaving us with a sense of awe and reverence, we are reminded of our place in the vastness of the cosmos.

We are but fleeting beings, caught in the ebb and flow of the universe's eternal dance.

CASSIOPEIA A

Deep within the stellar tapestry of
The constellation, Cassiopeia A emerges,
An impressive cosmic remnant.
A celestial portrait etched in scattered light,
Her brilliance transcends time.
A luminous tribute to celestial dances,
She whispers secrets of explosive demise,
Tales of cosmic rebirth, and boundless
Wonders woven throughout the universe's fabric.

COSMIC SONNET

Astronomers, they seek, and they explore,
    They journey far; they study deep and wide;
    The mysteries of space, its endless lore;
    And in their findings, the universe bides.
In the end, it's not just the facts they find,
    As they peer through their telescopes, lenses;
    Connection to the cosmos, unique kind,
    Glimpse of star births, wonder commences.
We are all astronomers in our way,
    Seeking stars, planets, constellations bright;
    And when we gaze upon the Milky Way,
    We know we are a part in every right.
In their light, we see ourselves reflected,
The universe, forever connected.

TWELVE COSMOLOGICAL WONDERS

Dark matter whispers,
　　a mysterious force weaving through galaxies.
Galaxies spin,
　　infinite ballets of celestial bodies.
Nebulas swirl,
　　vibrant canvases of interstellar art.
Solar eclipses mesmerize,
　　celestial dances of shadow and light.
Comets streak,
　　fleeting glimpses of cosmic beauty.
Solar flares ignite,
　　expelling fiery bursts of stellar energy.
Black holes devour,
　　swallowing light in boundless darkness.
Supernovas explode,
　　releasing the energy of a thousand suns.
Auroras dance,
　　painting polar skies with vibrant hues.
Satellites orbit,
　　sentinels over Earth's domain.
Constellations align,
　　telling stories of ancient mythology.
Cosmic microwave background hums,
　　echoes of the Big Bang.

TIME & MEMORIES

Time is a game played beautifully by children.
— HERACLITUS

TIME

AGE DEFYING

By shadows cast by fleeting time's cruel light,
She stands against the tides of aging's call,
A warrior in the battle for her might.

Lines etched upon her face, a silent fight,
Each wrinkle tells a story, rise and fall,
By shadows cast by fleeting time's cruel light.

Her hair, once dark, now fading to pure white,
A crown of wisdom in her graceful sprawl,
A warrior in the battle for her might.

Eyes, windows to a soul so strong, so bright,
Reflecting all the years, the highs, the stalls,
By shadows cast by fleeting time's cruel light.

She weaves her essence with a steady sight,
Resilient spirit breaking through the pall,
A warrior in the battle for her might.

With every breath, she conquers with delight,
Defying age's grasp, she stands tall,
By shadows cast by fleeting time's cruel light,
A warrior in the battle for her might.

A NEW YEAR

In the gentle embrace of the new year's dawn,
whispers of change dance upon the air.

It is a time of letting go,
of shedding the weight of the past,
and stepping into the embrace of new beginnings.

Like a delicate butterfly emerging from its cocoon,
we unfurl our wings and release memories
that have held us captive.

We bid farewell to the yesterdays that no longer serve us,
and burdens that have weighed heavily upon our hearts.

With each breath, we exhale the
sorrows, regrets, and what-ifs,
allowing them to dissipate into the ether.

For in this moment, we stand on
the precipice of possibility, ready to embrace
the unknown with open arms.

The canvas of the new year awaits our artistic touch,
eager to be painted with strokes of hope and dreams.

We gather the fragments of our
shattered past and transform them into
stepping stones toward a brighter future.

The lessons learned, tears shed, and battles fought

have shaped us into resilient beings,
capable of soaring to unimaginable heights.

As the sun rises on the first day of the year,
we celebrate the beauty of new beginnings.

Each day becomes
a symphony of possibilities,
an invitation to dance with life's melodies.

We raise our glasses to the endless opportunities
that lie ahead, to the doors waiting to be opened,
to the adventures yet to be embarked upon.

In this moment of renewal, we release chains of the
past and embrace the freedom of the present.

We allow ourselves to be vulnerable, to take risks,
to chase the dreams that have long lingered
in the depths of our souls.

For it is in the pursuit of our passions
that we find true fulfillment, and in the pursuit of our
dreams that we discover our purpose.

So let us toast to the new year, to the unwritten
chapters and blank pages that lay before us.

May we have the courage to let go of what
no longer serves us and the
strength to embrace the unknown.

Let us dance beneath the stars,
sing with the wind, and paint the world
with the vibrant colors of our dreams.

For in the tapestry of life, the past may be
woven into our story, but the future is ours to create.

GRIM

In the shrouded mist
Where silence reigns supreme,

A haunting figure materializes.
Draped in a cloak as black as midnight

The Grim Reaper, personification of Death,
Emerges from the depths of the unknown—

His presence sending chills through any witness.
Wrapped in a hood that obscures his face,

Concealing the mysteries that lie within
His silhouette, illuminated by a dim glow

Against the backdrop of a fog-laden landscape,
Casts an eerie ambiance upon the scene.

With an ethereal grace, the Reaper glides,
Sending tendrils of anticipation through the fog.

With bony hands, he wields a scythe,
A tool of finality and fate.

Gleaming with an ominous sheen,
Its blade softly sings of endings and transitions,

Reminding all who gaze upon it of the
Delicate balance between life and death.

As the Reaper traverses the misty veil, his dark cloak
Billows like the wings of a spectral creature,

Embracing the souls he guides into the great beyond,
A somber clue to the inevitability that awaits.

A reminder to live fully, love deeply,
While acknowledging life's fragility.

TIME PASSING

Time, a river flowing swift;
each passing day, a petal falls,
like autumn leaves, it drifts and shifts,
a symphony of murmurs, it enthralls.

A tick of the clock, a melody unrolled,
as time paints life's grand design;
the sun rises, dips, stories unfold,
a canvas of moments, forever enshrined.

TRANSTEMPORAL

lost in the currents of time
time travelers weave through

eras like yarn on
a cosmic loom

every step forward or back
woven into the fabric of existence

witnessing empires rise and crumble
love ignite and fade they are reminded

time is a river and
we are all but drifters

UNWRITTEN WORDS

Her heart wept for the
untold stories,
the unspoken truths,
the uncharted territories of
the human soul.

Her mind, a vast landscape of
unexplored realms,
beckoned her to wander
its labyrinthine corridors,
to unearth the buried
treasures of imagination.

As ever, the hour hand of the
clock ticked with cruel precision,
a constant reminder of her mortality,
stealing away the precious seconds,
minutes, and hours that remained.

Oh, how she yearned to chase
the wild winds of inspiration,
to dive into the depths of the
unknown and emerge with
tales that would ignite the hearts
of those who dared to listen.

Her words, like forgotten echoes,
whispered in her ear,
urging her to write faster,
to write with urgency,

for time was an unruly chariot,
wherein she was only a passenger
racing toward the precipice of eternity.

MEMORIES

BORN(E)

She carries the memories of childbirth
in the hushed corners of her mind,
like delicate whispers.
Each recollection, a thread
that weaves through the fabric
of her journey into motherhood.
As she closes her eyes, the images
dance before her, vivid and tender,
as if they were just yesterday.

She recalls the anticipation that
gripped her heart, mingled with the
anxious rhythm of her breath.
The long hours of labor, where
pain and determination fused
into a symphony of strength.
The room filled with a chorus of voices,
offering words of encouragement and love,
guiding her through tempestuous waves of sensation.

And then,
the crescendo of arrival.
The moment
when time stood still,
and she held her breath.
A torrent of emotions
flooded her being,
overwhelming and exhilarating.
In that instance, she emerged

as a vessel of life, transformed
by the miracle of creation.

As she cradled her daughter for the first time,
her trembling arms embraced a love so
profound, it defied description.
The weight of her newborn's fragile body
against her chest, the warmth of her skin
against her own, forged an unbreakable bond.
In that sacred space, the universe whispered
secrets only mothers know, and she vowed to
protect and cherish her child with every fiber of her being.

In the depth
of her memories,
she finds comfort and strength.
The indomitable spirit of motherhood,
a flame that burns brighter
with every passing day.
She holds onto those moments,
like precious treasures in the
recesses of her heart.
And as her daughter grows, she knows their
journey together will be woven with love,
resilience, and the enduring power of a mother's touch.

CRUNCHY DECADENCE

How my heart leaps with joy at the mere thought of you, my
sweet and indulgent delight.
It is not in the whispers of a lover's embrace that I find
comfort, but in the warm embrace of your tender crumb and
rich flavors; herein my truest affections lie.

I recall the first time our paths crossed, a serendipitous
encounter in a cozy bistro on a rainy evening.
The sight of you, glistening under the soft glow of
candlelight, beckoned me to taste your divine essence.
With each spoonful, I savored the delicate dance of pecans
and pralines, harmonizing in a symphony of flavors that left
me longing for more.

Then, one bustling holiday feast, you stood out on the
dessert table, adorned with a drizzle of bourbon sauce.
You were a sight to behold.
As I took my first bite, memories of festive gatherings and
shared laughter flooded my senses, intertwining with the
decadent sweetness of your essence.

On a lazy Sunday afternoon, seeking a moment of
tranquility, I found myself in the company of your delectable
form once more.
The velvety texture of your bread pudding, punctuated by
the crunch of caramelized pecans, was a symphony of
textures that delighted my palate.
With each mouthful, I felt a sense of contentment wash over
me, wrapped in the warmth of culinary bliss.

You, Pecan Praline Bread Pudding with Bourbon Sauce, are more than a dessert to me.
You are a keeper of memories, a source of comfort, and a reminder of life's simple pleasures.
In your sweetness and richness, I find fulfillment.

MUSIC'S POWER

There sits an elderly man, a silent pianist,
In a corner of a nursing home,
Where time lingers like a whisper in the air;
His fingers tremble on the keys of a past life.

Lost in the maze of memories slipping through his grasp,
He finds comfort in the language of music,
A language that needs no words, no memories,
Only raw emotion woven throughout its melody.

Notes, like delicate threads,
Weave a story of forgotten yesterdays,
Each key—a portal to a time long gone,
A time when memories were crystal clear.

The piano comes alive, singing a melancholic tune,
A symphony of forgotten dreams and faded hopes,
The man's eyes flicker with a spark of recognition,
A brief glimpse of a life once lived.

In that fleeting moment, time stands still,
The barriers of age and memory crumble,
And the music becomes a lifeline,
A bridge to a world lost in the fog of the past.

Silent witnesses to this ethereal dance,
Feel the music stir their dormant souls,
Awakening memories long buried,
And for a moment, they are young again.

The piano's lament echoes through corridors,
And shadows dance, reverberations of time,
Music is the healer, the storyteller,
A bright light in the darkness of forgetfulness.

REM SLEEP

As my bones find comfort
In the cocooning hour,
Beneath the soft embrace of my coverlet,
I sense the house
Exhale a weary sigh,
Its ancient timbers groaning
In the stillness of the night.

The whispers of memories
Linger in the shadows,
Echoes of laughter and tears
Imprinted in the walls.
The darkness becomes a canvas
For dreams to dance,
And I, a mere spectator
In the theater of slumber.
As the night unfolds its secrets,
I surrender to the symphony
Of silence and solitude,
Embracing the peace
That descends like a gentle mist
To cloak me in its comforting embrace.

In this tranquil realm of dreams,
Where time is but a fleeting wisp,
I journey through worlds unseen,
Exploring the depths of my soul.
Visions flicker like candle flames,
Illuminating hidden truths,
Unraveling mysteries long forgotten.

In the hushed embrace of night,
I find solace in the unknown,
Embracing the enigma of existence
And the infinite possibilities
That lie beyond the veil of consciousness.
As the stars twinkle in the velvet sky,
I drift deeper into the dream world,
Guided by the whispers of the night.

SWINGING

I envisioned myself
perched upon the swing at the
house nestled farther inland,
the house adorned with trees that
boasted vibrant trailing tropical vines,
while little lizards—their curious eyes
blinking in their interrogative way—
gracefully maneuvered up and down,
skillfully concealing themselves
amidst the dense foliage.

I saw my feet
securely tucked under to
prevent them from grazing
against the earth.
I bent my legs, using them as
leverage to propel
myself higher and higher,
my momentum increasing with each push.
It felt as though I was
soaring through the sky,
with the rush of wind and the
creak of the swing's rope on the sturdy tree branch,
harmonizing to lull me into a
state of meditative tranquility.

As I swung upwards,
I caught snapshots of the
azure heavens and fluffy clouds
adorning the arc of my ascent.

How I yearned to remain airborne,
to join the birds in their graceful flight.
Yet, gravity persistently tugged at me,
pulling me back toward the
opposite end of the swing's arc.
The ground seemed to vanish
beneath my feet as I bent my legs once more
and glimpsed the watchful eyes of two tiny lizards,
as the sky rushed toward me.

In that moment,
I closed my eyes,
stretched my legs out before me,
and gradually slowed my momentum.
I felt the atmosphere shift,
the air caressing my skin as it flowed past,
the ground rising steadily to meet me,
while the vines settled into a gentle sway,
recovering from the disturbed air
displaced by the swing,
with the dreaming girl who
wished she could fly.

TIME SLIPS

Oh, the man with a memory faded,
His mind slipping away, he's invaded,
Lost in the labyrinth of time,
Yet his past remains, a beacon that shines.

In the depths of a fog-filled mind,
His short-term memory slipping away,
A man once bright, now left behind,
Like a ghost that hides in the light of day.

Oh, the man with a memory faded,
His mind slipping away, he's invaded,
Lost in the labyrinth of time,
Yet his past remains, a beacon that shines.

He wanders through the halls of his mind,
But there, hidden among the cobwebs and dust,
Seeking solace he can no longer find,
Are memories of love, and in them, he'll trust.

Oh, the man with a memory faded,
His mind slipping away, he's invaded,
Lost in the labyrinth of time,
Yet his past remains, a beacon that shines.

He recalls the day he met his love,
Though her name eludes him, he feels her grace,
Underneath the stars, blessings from above,
In the warmth of his heart, her presence he'll embrace.

Oh, the man with a memory faded,
His mind slipping away, he's invaded,
Lost in the labyrinth of time,
Yet his past remains, a beacon that shines.

The man with dementia may forget his name,
The taste of his mother's homemade pie,
But the echoes of laughter, they still remain,
The twinkle in his father's weary eye.

Oh, the man with a memory faded,
His mind slipping away, he's invaded,
Lost in the labyrinth of time,
Yet his past remains, a beacon that shines.

And as the shadows grow longer each day,
We'll hold his hand, we'll be by his side,
And his memories slowly fade away,
As he takes his final journey, guided by love's light.

Oh, the man with a memory faded,
His mind slipping away, he's invaded,
Lost in the labyrinth of time,
Yet his past remains, a beacon that shines.

Though his short-term memory may have flown,
For the man with dementia, his legacy will last,
In the annals of his past, his spirit's shown,
In the hearts of those he loved, his memory held fast.

SEASONS & LIMINAL SPACES

Autumn is a second spring when every leaf is a flower.
—ALBERT CAMUS

SEASONS

AUTUMN'S EMBRACE

The woman stood in the stillness of her garden, her gaze fixed upon nature's artistry. The trees, once adorned in vibrant shades of green, now began their graceful transition into the resplendent embrace of autumn.

She watched as the leaves, like droplets of liquid amber and gold, slowly released their hold on slender branches. Each descent was a dance, a delicate pirouette, as they floated toward the earth, whispering secrets to the wind. The garden, once a sanctuary of lush greenery, now became a canvas of fiery hues and earthy tones.

As the sun bathed the garden in its warm glow, the woman felt the air grow crisp, carrying with it the scent of change. The summer's embrace loosened its grip, making way for the vivid arrival of autumn. She marveled at the resilience of nature, how effortlessly it adapted and transformed.

With each passing day, the colors intensified, as if the trees were determined to leave an indelible mark on the world before their temporary slumber. The fiery reds danced with the vibrant oranges, while the yellows shimmered like flecks of sunlight. The garden became a symphony of hues, a celebration of life's cyclical nature.

The woman found solace in this transition, in the fleeting beauty that nature bestowed upon her garden. She understood that change was inevitable, and that even in the act of transforming, there was a quiet strength that held everything together.

She observed the trees, their branches reaching toward the heavens, as if in an eternal embrace of the sky. The falling leaves became a gentle reminder of life's transience, urging her to cherish each fleeting moment, to embrace the beauty in impermanence.

With every breath, she reveled in the vibrant autumnal hues, knowing that within this transient beauty lay the seeds of rebirth, promising the arrival of a new season, and the eternal cycle of life.

GIVING THANKS

In the heart of a bustling city, where autumn lingered in the crisp air, there wandered a woman without a home, burdened by the weight of solitude and hunger. Her weary feet shuffled along the pavement, tracing a path through the alleyways adorned with crumbling bricks and forgotten dreams.

Her name, Judith, lost among the city's symphony of voices, was a mere echo in the wind. Her eyes, once vibrant emeralds, now dulled by the harsh reality of life on the streets. She wore tattered rags that clung to her frail form, affirming the relentless passage of time.

As the golden hues of autumn leaves danced above her, the woman yearned for comfort, a respite from the biting chill that gnawed at her bones. Thanksgiving approached, and with it, the promise of warmth and nourishment that seemed forever elusive.

Through the winding streets she wandered, her footsteps echoing tales of sorrow. Her search became a quest for not only sustenance, but for a flicker of hope amidst the shadows of her existence. She sought a place, a refuge, where a warm Thanksgiving meal awaited her, a feast that would momentarily mend the fragments of her broken spirit.

She stepped into a church, its wooden doors creaking open, revealing a sanctuary adorned with flickering candlelight.

The warmth embraced her, like a long-lost lover's embrace, as she sought solace within the hallowed walls.

The aroma of roasted turkey wafted through the air, mingling with the laughter and clinking of cutlery. In the dimly lit hall, tables stretched like a vast banquet, adorned with vibrant fruits and pies that whispered promises of sweet indulgence. Faces, both familiar and unfamiliar, gathered around, their eyes shining.

A gentle hand reached out, offering her a seat at the table, a place where she was no longer invisible. The woman without a home, her eyes brimming with gratitude, savored every morsel, felt a sense of belonging. She listened to the symphony of conversations, the laughter, and the stories told, woven like fragments of forgotten dreams finding their way back home.

In that moment, she remembered warmth was not merely the heat that emanated from a crackling hearth or the touch of a cozy blanket. It was the kindness of strangers, the generosity of a community, and the strength of the human spirit. And as the taste of pumpkin pie lingered on her lips, she found comfort in the empathetic and shared humanity.

NATURE'S CYCLE (A HAIKU CHAIN)

Roots dig deep in earth
Spring flowers bloom on the stem
Nature's cycle turns

Summer's heat beats down
Stem bends but flower still stands
Roots hold strong below

Autumn leaves fall fast
Flower's petals soon to go
Roots brace for winter

In the cold stillness
Roots wait hidden deep below
Spring's flower to grow

SEASONS

Time's hand turns in the cradle of eternity,
and the seasons dance their eternal waltz.
Spring, with her delicate touch, awakens
the slumbering earth from her wintry dream.
Her breath, a gentle zephyr, whispers
through the tender buds, coaxing them to bloom.
And the land, once adorned in a cloak of white,
is now painted in hues of pink and green.

Summer, the golden goddess, ascends
upon her throne of everlasting warmth.
Her rays, like molten honey, trickle down
to kiss the skin of both man and beast.
The world, ablaze with life, unfolds
in a grand tapestry of vibrant greens and blues.
And the air, scent heavy with blooming flowers,
sings a lullaby to the weary souls.

Autumn, the painter, takes his brush in hand
and strokes the landscape with fiery hues.
His palette, filled with amber and crimson,
creates a masterpiece of nature's farewell.
The trees, ablaze with colors, shed their leaves
in a graceful dance toward the waiting ground.
And the wind, a gentle whisperer of change,
whispers secrets of the approaching cold.

Winter, the ice queen, descends with grace
upon the world, her touch a frosty caress.
Her breath, a chilling breeze, freezes

the stillness of the land in icy embrace.
The earth, dressed in a cloak of white,
sleeps beneath a blanket of glistening snow.
And the silence, a hushed symphony of solitude,
invites reflection upon the cycles of life.

In this eternal waltz of the seasons,
the world dances to the melody of time.
Each season a chapter in nature's story,
each a testament to the beauty of change.
And as the earth turns and the seasons shift,
we marvel at the vivid tapestry of life,
knowing in every ending, a new beginning awaits,
and in every season, a glimpse of eternity.

SEPTEMBER SONG

It's another September.
And as days get shorter,
It's more difficult
To find time.

Then college football begins;
The teams and their records,
The games and the bowls,
The great comebacks
And overtime wins,
With young men
Dreaming of glory.

And for a few months
You will be distracted and find
Time a little slower,
Dragging its feet.

Each touchdown,
Each point scored,
A celebration of
Another season,
Another year.

SPRING AWAKENING

"Folded neatly," my mother said.

The sheets hang on the line
Smelling of warm
Spring sunshine and blossoms.

As I approach I see them
Alive, flapping in a sudden
Breeze, breathing in the
Fresh air,
Opening their
Pores to welcome the sun.

It seems a pity to take them down,
Suppress their joy.

I don't want to neatly fold.
I want to sit and enjoy
Their delight in the day.

WINTER'S GRACE NOTES

A mystical dance unfolds in the frosty world of winter's embrace, as snowflakes, like celestial messengers, descend from the heavens, each a unique creation, a miniature masterpiece, divinely designed. They twirl and pirouette through the air, their delicate forms glistening in the pale moonlight, weaving threads of frozen wonder across the land.

The world, cloaked in a pristine robe of white, becomes a sanctuary—serene, sounds muffled. Trees stand tall and proud, their branches adorned with delicate icicles, crystal chandeliers that shimmer and sparkle with every gust of wind. The ground is a canvas of untouched purity, a blank slate inviting us to leave our mark, imprint our dreams upon its frozen surface.

The snow crunches beneath our feet with every step, a symphony of sound, a thousand secrets shared. The air is crisp and invigorating, filling our lungs with icy breaths, awakening our senses, and reminding us of beauty in the simplest of moments.

As the winter solstice approaches, we gather together, bound by the warmth of our love and the light of our spirits. Many of us light fires that flicker and dance in the hearth, casting shadows upon the walls as we huddle close, seeking comfort in each other's company. The solstice reminds us that even in the darkest times, there is always a glimmer of hope, a promise of light.

As the solstice passes, we emerge from the darkness, like the phoenix rising from the ashes, ready to embrace the world with renewed vigor and hearts filled with love. Some of us gather under starlit skies, raising our voices in song, and we discover melodies that transcend time and space and carry our hopes and dreams into the universe. The stillness of night, broken by our harmonious chorus, becomes a celebration of life and all its wonders.

Families gather, their hearts alight with joy, exchanging tokens of love and gratitude. Each carefully wrapped gift holds within it a piece of our hearts, a tangible reminder of our love and appreciation for one another. We revel in the joy of seeing smiles light up faces, of witnessing the pure delight that comes with unwrapping the mysteries of the world. Gifts, like winter's other grace notes, are woven into the fabric of this season, highlighting the beauty of human connection.

Beyond the material treasures, we find ourselves immersed in the true gift of winter: a time of reflection and introspection, a chance to turn inward and nurture our souls. For in the harshest of seasons—as the world remains frozen in time, awaiting Spring's first gentle touch—we may find the strength to endure and cherish the warmth within us, learn to appreciate the fleeting beauty of a snowflake, the soft crackle of a fire, and the embrace of loved ones.

LIMINAL SPACES

A HAUNTING

A haunting presence, lurking in the mist,
As moonlight fades, their grip continues.
Through the darkness, their whispers exist,
In the misty veil, their secrets prevail.

As moonlight fades, their grip continues,
Unseen forces, turning and writhing.
In the misty veil, their secrets prevail,
A web of fear, forever turbulent.

Unseen forces, turning and writhing,
Nightmares woven in midnight tapestry.
A web of fear, forever turbulent,
Their presence looms, casting dark light.

Nightmares woven in midnight tapestry,
They prey upon the unsuspecting spirit.
Their presence looms, casting dark light,
Concealed within the shadows they control.

They prey upon the unsuspecting spirit,
A dance of terror, a macabre act.
Concealed within the shadows they control,
Their haunting laughter turning heads.

A dance of terror, a macabre act,
In this realm of fear, they hold power.
Their haunting laughter turning heads,
Leading lost souls further away.

In this realm of fear, they hold power,
Whispering secrets, fueling despair.
Leading lost souls further away,
Their grip tightens, a suffocating snare.

Whispering secrets, fueling despair,
Their presence lingers, an eternal darkness.
Their grip tightens, a suffocating snare,
In the depths of dark, they ignite.

Their presence lingers, an eternal darkness,
Shrouded in night, their essence flourishes.
In the depths of dark, they ignite,
As fear consumes, no one survives.

Shrouded in night, their essence flourishes,
A haunting poem, a chilling tale.
As fear consumes, no one survives,
In the deepest dark, they shall prevail.

A haunting poem, a chilling tale,
A haunting presence, lurking in the mist.
In the deepest dark, they shall prevail,
Through the darkness, their whispers exist.

ANANCY

Where ancient trees whisper secrets,
And rivers flow with stories yet untold,
In the heart of a lush Jamaica,
There dwells Anancy, the cunning spider.

With eight nimble legs,
And eyes that miss nothing,
Anancy weaves his web of mischief,
A trickster, a master of deception.

Shape-shifter of the shadows,
He moves with a sly smile,
A mysterious figure,
Wise and enigmatic.

In the dance of tropical light,
Anancy spins his tales,
Transforming from spider to man,
A weaver of intricate schemes.

Anancy the spider first did rise,
Among the Akan people,
In Africa's vibrant lands,
With cunning wit, clever guise.

From Ghana's shores, his tales did sail,
Through the dark and harrowing seas,
Of the transatlantic slave trade's plight,
To the Caribbean's luxuriant shores.

Anancy, a swindler bold and sly,
Symbol of wit that could resist,
The chains of bondage, the weight of grief,
Through stories spun, offering release.

Through hardships faced, his wisdom shone,
Lessons taught in a playful timbre,
Resilience, resourcefulness, and art,
In Anancy's tales, pulsating, alive.

Passed down through generations long,
In oral traditions, a timeless call,
Each storyteller adding their part,
To Anancy's lore, a skillful work.

A cultural hero, a bold figure,
In African and Caribbean lands,
Anancy weaves his storied web,
A legacy that will never grow old.

In the echoes of his clever schemes,
In the laughter of his playful fantasies,
Anancy lives on, in tales forever,
In the hearts of those who adore his lore.

AN OTHERWORLDLY REALM

Hidden amongst the gnarled trees and moss-covered stones,
in the depths of an ancient forest, lay a portal.

It shimmered with an otherworldly luminescence,
beckoning curious souls who dared to venture close.

As one stepped through the portal,
reality shifted and transformed.

The air crackled with magic, and the landscape
transformed into an ethereal realm.

Floating islands suspended in the sky,
adorned with cascading waterfalls and vibrant flora.

Mythical creatures roamed freely,
wings brushing against the wisps of floating clouds.

Time lost its meaning, and the boundaries
between dreams and reality blurred.

This portal, a gateway to an enchanting world,
offered a glimpse into a fantastical kingdom,
a journey into the limitless worlds of imagination.

SURREALITY

Where dreams dance with reality, there exists a garden of
whispers.
Each petal of the flowers holds a secret, a tale of forgotten
melodies.
The sun, a golden coin in the sky, casts shadows that speak
in tongues unknown to mortal ears.

Amidst the swirling mists of time, a lone figure walks with
feet that leave no imprint on the soft grass.
Their eyes, two pools of liquid moonlight, reflect the
universe's secrets.
They reach out to touch a butterfly made of stardust, its
wings shimmering with galaxies yet to be born.

The trees in this ethereal garden hum ancient lullabies, their
branches swaying in harmony with the cosmic symphony.
The breeze carries echoes of lost memories, whispers of
what once was and what could be.
Time itself bends and weaves, creating patterns only the
heart can decipher.

In this surreal existence, where reality and fantasy blend
seamlessly, the boundaries of the mind dissolve.
Here, in the garden of whispers, the soul finds comfort, the
spirit finds freedom, and the essence of being is laid bare
under the watchful gaze of the eternal stars.

THE EDGES

I am fascinated with "edges," all those natural transitional spaces.

I am drawn to the plants at the edge or border of a garden in the sun, where the shorter plants offer a profusion of blooms to attract the bees and butterflies.

I am drawn to the gardens in the dappled shade of the trees transitioning to the woods, where shade-loving plants offer cover for butterflies and insects, crows build nests in tall oaks, and squirrels clean themselves of mites with a roll in the cool earth.

I am drawn to the woods behind our house that back up to farmland, to that space where shade-loving trees meet sun-loving grasses, where the groundhog hibernates in its burrow, the fox has a den, and the chipmunks hide their winter store.

I am drawn to the water's edge when we visit the beach in the summer, where the waves hypnotically push and pull the sand, and the sand crabs, roly-polies, and beach hoppers live.

I am drawn to the shoreline—the boundary between the land, sand, and water—where seagulls hunt the fish in the shallow waters of tide pools, and shellfish and mollusks attach themselves to rocks, docks, marinas, and boats.

I am drawn to the dawn, a twilight in reverse, when the blurred edges of night give way to the bright light-focused rays of the sun, when the mother fox creeps back to her den of kits, and the birds begin their morning serenade.

I am drawn to twilight, when bats emerge to eat their fill of the night insects, when frogs, toads, and peepers begin their evening concert, and fireflies begin their courtship of blinking lights in late June.

You see, ecosystems meet at the edges, creating diverse habitats, acting as buffers for nature's wrath, and contributing to the resilience and stability of the environment.

And if you are at all spiritual, it is at the edges where the inner being meets the corporeal, where questions are answered, and where true communion begins.

THE MACABRE

Lost within the darkest
Corners of my mind,
The spirit of Edgar Allan Poe
Holds sway haunting my every thought.

Like a raven's shadow,
His words flutter through
My mind's labyrinthine streets,
Whispering tales of sorrow, despair.

His stories,
Fragmented dreams,
Unfold before my eyes,
Each word a haunting melody.

With each turn of phrase,
He conjures images of blackened
Hearts, twisted souls, painting
A portrait in shades of anguish, melancholy.

His pen, a quill dipped
In the blood of the damned,
Engraves lines of poetry that
Pierces the very fabric of reality.

I become entangled in the
Web of his words, unable to
Break free from the grip of
His macabre enchantment.

OBSERVATIONS & VIEWS

The world is full of magical things patiently waiting for our wits to grow sharper.

—BERTRAND RUSSELL

OBSERVATIONS

ALL THAT JAZZ

With the haze of cigarette smoke and dimly lit ambiance,
the jazz club becomes a sanctuary of sound,
where the music weaves a spell of enchantment,
drawing us into its world of improvisation and soul.

Each musician a storyteller,
their instruments speaking a language of emotion,
painting vivid landscapes of joy and sorrow,
echoing the highs and lows of the human experience.

The audience becomes a part of the performance,
their hearts beating in time with the music,
their spirits lifted by the melodies that soar,
and their souls touched by the raw, unfiltered truth.

In this sacred space of creative expression,
where notes hang in the air like shimmering stars,
we find solace in the midst of chaos,
and connection in the shared experience of music.

As the last note fades into the night,
and the echoes of applause fill the room,
we are left with a sense of wonder and gratitude,
knowing that in this moment, we were truly alive.

BASKETBALL DREAMS

In the dimly lit gymnasium, where the echoes of bouncing basketballs and the cheers of fervent spectators entwine, she stands tall. A woman of determination and unwavering passion, she gazes upon the court, her eyes ablaze with a fire that has burned since her earliest memories.

With each dribble, she dances with the ball, her feet moving gracefully, guided by years of practice and an unyielding love for the game. The court becomes her stage, and the rhythm of her heart beats in sync with the swish of the net.

She recalls the days of her youth, where dreams were forged in the crucible of her imagination. When others laughed and dismissed her lofty ambitions, she persisted, fueled by a spirit that refused to be subdued. And now, she stands here, in the world of her childhood dreams, wearing the jersey that bears her name, evidence of her unwavering dedication.

The crowd roars in adulation, their voices blending into a symphony of support. With each basket she scores, the cheers grow louder, as if the universe itself is applauding her triumph. She is an inspiration, a symbol of what can be achieved when dreams are pursued with fervor and determination.

Beneath the glow of the spotlight, a humbleness resides within her. She knows that the path to this moment was not one she walked alone. It was paved by the sacrifices of loved ones, the guidance of mentors, and the unwavering belief in herself. The weight of their faith rests on her shoulders, propelling her forward, even when doubt threatens to cloud her mind.

In her presence, the court becomes a canvas, and every move she makes is a brushstroke, painting a picture of her journey. The fluidity of her motions tells a story of determination, resilience, and the unyielding spirit of a woman who has shattered barriers with a ball in her hand.

As the final buzzer sounds, and the game draws to a close, she takes a moment to absorb the magnitude of her achievement. The victory is not just for her, but for every little girl who has ever dared to dream beyond the limitations imposed by society. She stands as proof of the power of perseverance, inspiring a generation to reach for the stars, no matter the obstacles that lie in their path.

With a humble smile and a heart filled with gratitude, she steps off the court, knowing that her journey has only just begun. The legacy she leaves behind will forever echo in the hearts of those who witnessed her greatness. For she is not just a basketball player, but a symbol of the indomitable spirit that resides within us all, waiting to be unleashed.

FROM SUN TO SNOW

1.
By the cerulean waters of the Caribbean,
where the gentle currents weave tales
of resilience and adventure,
there lived a woman whose roots ran deep,
anchoring her to a land of sun-kissed
shores and vibrant traditions.
A daughter of the Cayman Islands,
her family's legacy is
entwined with the very
essence of the sea.

Generations before her,
her grandfather and great-grandfather
were captains of ships,
navigators of the unknown,
charting their course through
the vast expanse of the ocean.
Their tales echoed through her childhood,
whispered in the rustling palms and
carried by the trade winds that caressed her skin.
The sea was a part of her,
flowing through her veins
like the rhythm of a distant drum.

It was her grandfather, Captain James,
who first ignited the spark of the sea within her.
Tales of his voyages would
fill her childhood nights,
painting vivid pictures of distant

lands and endless horizons.
With every story, her heart yearned
to explore the uncharted waters,
to taste the salt on her lips, and
to feel the wind caress her
face as it did her forefathers.

2.
And so, the sea called to her, its
siren song echoing through her soul.
She embarked on her own voyage,
not on a ship, but through the pages of history,
tracing her family's footsteps across time.
She discovered her great-grandfather,
Captain William, who sailed the
Caribbean during the golden age of piracy.
He was a man of honor, his ship a
beacon of hope for those seeking
safety from marauders.

Her love for the sea was eternally
entwined with her love for her homeland.
The Cayman Islands, with their
crystal-clear waters and coral reefs,
had become a part of her very essence.
She would often sit by the shore,
her toes sinking into the warm sand, and
gaze at the horizon, where the sky and
sea became one.
In those moments, she felt the
spirit of her ancestors,
their power and resilience
coursing through her veins.

3.
She felt elated as she uncovered

forgotten tales of bravery and strength,
stories woven into the very fabric of her existence.
She imagined her ancestors
battling treacherous storms,
guiding their ships with unwavering determination.
She could almost hear their voices
whispering in the wind,
Pointing her toward her destiny.

With every breath she took, the
Caribbean air filled her lungs with the
essence of her heritage.
The taste of coconut and spices
mingled on her tongue, transporting
her to the bustling markets of George Town,
where her family had once traded their treasures.
The vibrant colors of the islands
danced before her eyes,
etching a kaleidoscope of
memories on her mind.

4.
But fate had a different voyage
in store for her,
as her husband's company,
a behemoth in the world of finance,
summoned him to Nova Scotia, Canada—
a place far colder than any she had ever known.
The thought of leaving her beloved Cayman Islands,
with its golden beaches and sapphire horizons,
filled her with anxiety and trepidation.
She felt herself becoming unmoored,
as the impending departure felt like an
unraveling of the tether to her ancestral home.

As they arrived in Nova Scotia,

the biting winds
swept away any lingering warmth,
leaving her shivering in a foreign land.
The people spoke with a different cadence,
their words punctuated by
the crispness of the air.
When they arrived, it was to
a land of snow-laden
forests, frozen lakes, and icy shores—
a stark contrast to the
vibrant colors of her island home.

5.

In the early days, she clung to her
Caymanian identity like a
buoy adrift in unfamiliar waters.
She sought solace in her
family's tales of adventure,
their voyages to distant lands, and
the treasures they had brought back.
As she walked along the frozen
shores of Nova Scotia,
she yearned for the sound of lapping
waves and the embrace of the sun's warmth.

She immersed herself in the local culture,
learning the Gaelic melodies that
echoed through the highlands,
and reveled in the
hearty warmth of a Halifax
donair on a chilly winter's night.
She embraced her own Scottish
ancestry, the seafarers, who traveled
to this very land, who traveled
to the Caribbean, leaving Scotland forever,
to live and flourish on a foreign shore.

6.

Now, she had done the same,
traveling to a distant land, to
New Scotland, a land that slowly
began to wend its ways into her heart,
the land slowly revealing its secrets to her,
its hidden beauty emerging from
beneath the layers of snow.
As the icy grip of winter began to thaw,
replaced by the delicate blossoms of spring,
she found herself discovering
a new sense of belonging.

The seasons danced through the years,
and she discovered a strength that
lay dormant within her.
She built a community,
kindred spirits who had come
to this foreign land, each displaced
but determined to create new dreams.
Their shared experiences wove a
strong bond of support, one that
lifted them up, kept them afloat
above the longing that at times
threatened to overwhelm them.

7.

Though her heart would forever yearn
for the Cayman Islands,
the tides of life had carried her to
this distant shore.
As she reflected upon her journey,
she realized that the legacy of
her family's seafaring spirit
still coursed through her veins.

The same determination that had
guided her ancestors through
uncharted waters now propelled her forward,
to embrace new challenges and triumphs.

IN HOSPITAL

The sterile walls seemed to close in as
Machines hummed with a steady rhythm.
The scent of antiseptic mingled with the
Smell of spent flowers brought by well-wishers.
Soft sunlight filtered through the blinds,
Casting a gentle glow upon the room.
Nurses spoke in hushed voices,
Reverence for death's delicate dance.
The woman in the bed, her face etched with
Lines of years and pain smiled gently.
Loved ones gathered around, whispering
Prayers of intercession, asking for a miracle.
Her regrets wilted as a moment of gratitude bloomed.

PLASTICS

The once pristine waters that flowed freely through the rivers and oceans now carry a heavy burden of plastic waste. The vibrant hues of blue and green are marred by floating debris, a stark reminder of humanity's careless disregard for the environment.

In the depths of the ocean, where mysterious creatures once thrived, plastic now lurked like a silent predator. Sea turtles mistake plastic bags for jellyfish, swallowing them whole and facing a slow and painful death. Dolphins and whales become entangled in discarded fishing nets, their freedom stolen by the invisible traps lurking beneath the waves.

The delicate balance of the underwater ecosystem is disrupted as plastic invades every corner of the ocean. Coral reefs, once teeming with life, now struggle to survive under the weight of plastic pollution. The colorful fish that darts among the coral are now forced to navigate through a sea of plastic waste, their habitats shrinking with each passing day.

Above the surface, rivers carry a similar burden of plastic waste, choking the life out of the waterways. Birds that once soared gracefully over the rivers now find themselves tangled in plastic six-pack rings, their wings unable to carry them to safety. Fish struggle to navigate through the murky waters, their scales coated in a toxic layer of microplastics.

The impact of plastic pollution extends beyond the creatures that call the waterways home. The environment itself suffers as plastic waste leaches harmful chemicals into the water, contaminating the very source of life. The health of the planet is in jeopardy, as plastic waste accumulates at an alarming rate, suffocating the natural world in its synthetic embrace.

For the inhabitants of the planet, especially those who rely on water-dwelling creatures for sustenance, the consequences are dire. Fishermen pull up nets filled not with fish, but with plastic debris, their livelihoods threatened by the pollution that now infest the waters. Those who consume seafood unknowingly ingest microplastics, a toxic legacy of humanity's disregard for the health of the planet.

As the waters grow darker with each passing day, the need for action becomes more urgent. The cries of the creatures that call the oceans and rivers home echo through the polluted waters, a haunting reminder of the price of our indifference.

SEA WORTHY

 Souls adrift,
lost in a vast expanse,
hopes and dreams
swallowed by unforgiving waves.

Mothers, fathers,
eyes wild with desperation,
clutch children to their chests,
praying for an improbable miracle.

The sea, a hungry beast,
devours their hopes and dreams,
leaving nothing but the
bitter taste of salt and despair.

Babies cry out in terror,
tiny fingers grasp for
anything that might
save them.

But there is nothing,
only the sea's endless expanse
that stretches before them
swallows them whole.

The sun beats down,
harsh, suffocating;
they thirst for relief
that is nonexistent.

They are adrift,
lost
in a sea of
hopelessness.

Still they fight to exist,
struggling for every breath,
every pulsation,
heroes in an unwinnable battle.

But, the sea is unrelenting;
its waves crash against
battered bodies,
dragging them into the abyss.

They scream
in agony,
voices lost
in the sea's roar.

Then silence echoes across
the sea's vastness,
silence that speaks of horror
and the desperation of ones who perish.

The sea claims its victims,
leaving nothing but
memories of brave souls,
fighting for their lives.

SERENDIPITY

Shadows danced with the soft notes of jazz,
In the hushed embrace of the hotel bar,
A lone figure in a sea of fleeting faces,
Heart heavy with the weight of disappointment.

Dry martini in hand, a bitter companion,
Its cool touch fleeting comfort against the ache within.
Stood up, abandoned in a crowd of strangers,
Seeking refuge in the amber glow of the bar's lights.

Then you appeared bar side, a gentle presence,
With eyes that held a universe of understanding,
Your voice a soothing melody for chaotic thoughts,
A lifeline thrown in the stormy sea of emotions.

Your words wove a tapestry of shared sorrows and joys,
Threads of laughter and empathy stitching them together,
In the quiet intimacy of that dimly lit sanctuary,
Your souls found solace in each other's company.

As the night deepened, time became a fleeting whisper,
Your connection growing stronger with each shared
moment,
A blossoming bond that defied the boundaries of reason,
A serendipitous encounter that felt like destiny's gentle hand.

And in the stillness of the midnight hour,
You knew, with a certainty that transcended words,
That this meeting was more than mere chance,

It was the beginning of a love story written in the stars.

A story painted in hues of vulnerability and strength,
Brushstrokes of resilience and acceptance,
Your hearts beating in synchrony, a rhythm of newfound hope,
A melody of connection that resonated deep within your souls.

In the quiet depths of the hotel bar,
Where time seemed to stand still in reverence,
You found yourselves lost in a dance,
Of shared experiences and unspoken truths.

The world outside faded into insignificance,
As you delved into the depths of each other's hearts,
Unveiling layers of fears and dreams,
Embracing the flaws and scars that made you whole.

And, as the night waned, giving way to the first light of dawn,
Your laughter echoed through the empty bar,
A symphony of joy and possibility,
A prelude to a future in love's embrace.

Hand in hand, you walked out into the quiet morning,
The world around you bathed in the soft glow of a new day,
Your hearts connected in a silent promise,
To navigate the uncertainties of life together, come what may.

When you stepped into the dawn of a new beginning,
You knew that in each other,
You had found the missing piece of your souls,
A love that had bloomed from the ashes of past sorrows.

For in that hotel bar where fate had steered you,
You discovered a love as timeless as the cosmos,
A love that would weather the storms of life,
Guided by the unwavering light of your hearts.

THE IMMIGRANT

She arrived, a woman of Caribbean breezes,
In a bustling city's symphonic resonance;
Her skin a canvas painted by the sun's caress,
Eyes carrying the depth of ocean mysteries.

She became a pebble in a mighty river's flow,
Caught between white and black currents;
Curiosity and assumptions enveloped her,
An outsider in the landscape of dualities.

The white Americans, eyes wide with wonder,
Seeking to place her in their familiar boxes,
Assuming her origins from South America,
Compliments masking ignorance, missing her essence.

The black Americans, eyes filled with skepticism,
Questioning her connection to shared struggles,
Doubting the authenticity of her journey,
A sense of not quite belonging.

She, in her quest for acceptance,
Begins to mold herself to blend in,
Straightening her hair, softening her accent,
Wearing masks that dimmed her vibrant spirit.

But one day, at the crossroads of identity,
She stood before the mirror, a reflection staring back,
Of a strong woman, roots deep in ancestral soil,
And a decision sparked, a transformation ignited.

Curls of hair reclaimed their natural glory,
Accent reverberating with the island's cadence,
Colors of the Caribbean adorned her being,
Authenticity unfurled, unapologetically radiant.

Stares and whispers lost their cutting edge,
She stood tall, grounded in her truth,
Stories spilled like rivers from her lips,
Laughter echoing like waves against the shore.

Bridging the chasms between cultures,
She became an authentic tapestry,
Woven from the multicolored threads of her heritage,
A mosaic piece fitting seamlessly in the city's fabric.

Belonging, not in fitting into predefined molds,
But in standing boldly in the light of her truth,
In embracing her Caribbean roots with pride,
A home found in the hearts that saw her essence.

She was a woman reborn in the embrace of self,
A sister in spirit to those who saw beyond labels,
Standing in the light of her own truth,
A living poem of resilience and grace in a world of
conformity.

VENETIAN DREAMS

I've visited Venice several times in my dreams, whimsical journeys to an enchanting city.

Dreams that unveiled surreal scenes, where the city's canals were filled with swirling waters, flooding the narrow streets as I stood upon elevated walkways, gazing down at the rippling reflections of the ornate buildings.

Here, gondolas glided gracefully through the labyrinth of waterways, their sleek forms cutting through the depths like graceful swans. The gondoliers, with their striped shirts and straw hats, skillfully maneuvered the boats, guiding them along the submerged streets.

Mesmerized, my eyes beheld the Bridge of Sighs, its arches reflected in the shimmering waters below. Legend whispered that it held the sighs and sorrows of lovers, forever trapped within its stone walls, a melancholic symbol of longing and lost love.

As I wandered through the dream-Venice, I stumbled upon the majestic domes and spires that adorned the city's skyline. Each architectural masterpiece seemed to reach for the heavens, as if longing to touch the clouds themselves. The grandeur of St. Mark's Basilica and the intricacy of the Doge's Palace left me awestruck, their beauty transcending the boundaries of my imagination.

The dream carried me to bustling plazas, where the carnival spirit danced in the air. The vibrant colors of masquerade masks and elaborate costumes painted the scene with a kaleidoscope of hues. Laughter and music filled the streets, blending with the salty sea air that wrapped the city in its embrace.

In this ethereal dream of Venice, I became one with the city's essence. I felt the ebb and flow of its tides within my soul, the rhythm of the canals pulsating through my veins. It was a dream where reality and fantasy intertwined, where the beauty of the city merged with the depths of my imagination.

As the dream slowly faded, I longed to return to Venice's embrace once more, to wander through its flooded streets, to drift along the canals in a gondola, and to savor the magic of this dreamlike city.

VIEWS

CHOICE

Where the pulse of democracy beats,
Shadows of uncertainty loom large,
Casting a somber hue
Over the impending elections,
A pivotal moment in time.

A figure of strength and resilience,
Stands at the forefront of one ticket,
A former prosecutor with a voice that echoes justice.
Her roots span the seas and continents,
Caribbean American and Indian American,
A tapestry woven with threads of diversity and hope.

On the opposing end of the spectrum,
A figure shrouded in controversy,
A convicted felon with a shadowed past.
Allegations of heinous crimes and misdeeds
Paint a portrait of a man at odds with integrity,
An adjudicated rapist whose presence
Taints the political landscape.

The dichotomy between these two figures
Reflects a nation at a crossroads,
Torn between ideals of progress and regression.
The fate of democracy hangs in the balance,
A choice between light and darkness,
The light of democracy or the
Darkness of authoritarianism,
Hope and despair.

The corridors of power and the
Streets of every town pulsate with the
Urgency of democracy,
Each vote a declaration of
Allegiance to foundational principles.

This election is not just a
Political event but a moral crossroads,
Shaping the country's future and
Character for years to come.

As the nation grapples with its conscience,
The echoes of the people's voices
Resonate with the weight of history,
A reminder of the power and responsibility
That rests in the hands of the electorate.

HATE RISES

Whispers of a dark past linger,
In the quiet corners of memory;
Shadows of hatred casting long
Echoes of fear reverberate.

The rise of Nazi sentiments,
A chilling specter haunting lands,
Europe and America, conjoined,
In the grip of intolerance's hand.

What does this mean,
But a resurgence of the old
Ideologies of division and despair,
Threads of prejudice woven anew?

It portends a storm brewing;
Clouds of xenophobia gathering,
Lightning strikes of extremism,
Thunderous echoes of authoritarianism.

How can it be combatted,
This venomous spread of hate,
With words as weapons, wielded,
In the battle for hearts and minds?

Education, the light in darkness,
Knowledge to dispel ignorance,
Awareness to break the chains,
Unity to mend the fractures.

Stand against the tide of hate,
Raise voices in solidarity,
Champion the cause of justice,
Defend the rights of all.

In the fabric of humanity,
Threads of diversity entwine,
Colors of difference paint a picture,
Of resilience, of strength, of hope.

Combat the rise of shadows,
With the light of understanding,
Illuminate the path to empathy,
Embrace the beauty of difference.

For in the struggle against hate,
In the fight for a brighter tomorrow,
We find the essence of humanity,
In unity, in love, in peace.

IMMUNITY

Where the scales of truth and power sway,
In the hallowed chambers of justice,
A ruling was cast like a stone into the still waters,
Creating ripples that echoed through the land.

The Supreme Court's gavel fell,
And with it, the essence of democracy trembled,
As a cloak of immunity was draped upon the President,
Shielding official criminal acts from the grasp of justice.

A veil of uncertainty descended,
Shrouding the nation in a haze of fear and doubt,
Whispers of dissent mingling with the cries of protest,
In a symphony of resistance against the tyranny of power.

The threads of justice, once woven strong,
Now frayed and fragile in the face of impunity,
As the heart of democracy beat with a hesitant rhythm,
Questioning the very foundation on which it stood.

In the shadow of a ruling that defied reason,
Courage rose like a phoenix from the ashes of despair,
Voices raised in defiance, hands clasped in unity,
A mosaic of hope painted on the canvas of resistance.

In the corridors of power, where shadows whispered of
corruption,
There were those who dared to speak truth to power,
Their words cutting through the darkness like a sharpened
blade,

Exposing the cracks in the facade of impunity.

And in the hearts of the people, a seed of hope blossomed,
Nurtured by the collective will to stand firm in the face of
adversity,
To fight for a future where justice prevails,
Where the echoes of truth resonate louder than the whispers
of tyranny.

For in the crucible of challenge and trial,
It is in the resilience of the human spirit that true strength
lies,
A strength that withstands the test of time,
A strength that lights the way toward a brighter tomorrow.

MEDIA WEAPONIZED

The right seized upon
a powerful weapon to
shape narratives and
control minds: the media.

Like puppet masters
pulling invisible strings,
they spun tales of
deception and manipulation,
weaving a web of
half-truths and falsehoods to
confuse and control the masses.

Through a cacophony of
voices that drowned out dissent,
they crafted a distorted reality
where truth became subjective
and facts were malleable.

The lines between news and
propaganda blurred,
as sensationalism and
fear-mongering became tools
of coercion and influence.

In the echo chambers of
social media and news outlets,
the right wielded the media
like a double-edged sword,
cutting through reason and
critical thinking to serve their

own agenda of power and control.

SHADOWS OF AUTHORITARIANISM

A shadow loomed over the land,
casting a chilling darkness that
crept into people's hearts.

The rise of authoritarianism,
like a malignant weed,
spread its roots deep into the soil of democracy,
choking the voices of dissent and
sowing seeds of fear and compliance.

Leaders once hailed as guardians of freedom
now wielded power like a weapon,
crushing opposition and dissent with an iron fist.

The pillars of justice and democracy
trembled in the face of tyranny,
as the populace watched in silent horror,
afraid to speak out against the encroaching darkness.

In the halls of power, the echoes of oppression reverberated,
a grim reminder of the fragility of liberty in the face of
unchecked authority.

STALKING FREEDOM

We call it the land of the free,
where dreams are born and ideals are
woven into the tapestry of the nation,
where a shadow stretches
across the landscape.

It is the shadow of guns,
of violence unchained,
of lives cut short in the blink of an eye.

Schools stand as silent witnesses
to the horror, their walls echoing
with the cries of children who
should be learning and laughing,
not cowering in fear.

The innocence of youth shattered
by the crack of gunfire,
leaving scars that may never fully heal.

Grocery stores, once bustling
with the hum of everyday life,
now bear the weight of tragedy.

Aisles once filled with the mundane
necessities of existence now
stained with blood, a stark reminder of
how quickly normalcy can be
shattered by the deadly pull of a trigger.

At gatherings meant for joy and unity,
lurks a sense of unease, a knowledge
that in this age of uncertainty,
no place is truly safe.

Celebrations turn into memorials,
laughter into tears, as the specter of
gun violence looms over every crowd, every event,
casting a pall of fear over the collective consciousness.

The Second Amendment,
a relic of a bygone era,
now stands as a battleground
in the war for the soul of a nation.

Did the founding fathers envision a future
where the right to bear arms would lead
to a culture of violence, where the very weapons
meant for protection would become instruments of
destruction?

Common sense gun legislation,
a phrase whispered in the halls of
power and shouted in the streets,
remains an elusive dream.

The call to outlaw certain types of automatic
weapons is met with resistance, with arguments
that echo through chambers of government and
across the divide of public opinion.

What will it take to bring about change,
to stem the tide of violence that washes over the land?

It will take courage, the kind that stands firm in the face of
adversity,

that refuses to back down in the face of opposition.

It will take empathy, the ability to see beyond
personal interests and toward the greater good,
to understand that the right to life should always
supersede the right to own weapons of war.

In the silence that follows each tragedy,
there is a call to action, a plea for change
that reverberates through the
collective consciousness.

The path to common sense gun legislation
is fraught with obstacles,
with voices raised in protest and in support,
each side entrenched in their beliefs.

Yet, there, a glimmer of hope,
a flicker of light that pierces
through the darkness.
It is the hope that one day, the shadow of guns
will recede, and the nation will emerge into a new dawn,
where the right to live in safety and security
is cherished above all else.

ERODED

With promises of equality and progress,
in a nation vibrant with freedom,
the rights of women began to wither,
like petals in the harsh wind of change.

Laws that once safeguarded our
autonomy and choices, chipped away,
one by one, by the hands of those who sought
to diminish voices of half the population.

The sanctity of our bodies, once held sacred,
now faced scrutiny and control from forces
that sought to dictate what we could and
could not do with our own flesh and blood.

The battleground for our rights shifted
from courtrooms to legislative chambers,
where decisions that shaped our
futures were made without our consent.

With each passing day, the silken threads
of our rights grow thinner, leaving behind
a stark reminder of the fragility of progress.

WOUNDS & CONTEMPLATIONS

The wound is the place where the light gets in.

—RUMI

WOUNDS

DEPRESSION

In the depths of sorrow, she finds no peace,
A young girl lost in shadows of her mind,
Her spirit trapped in darkness, seeking release.

Each day a battle that refuses to cease,
Her heart weighed down, a heavy burden bind,
In the depths of sorrow, she finds no peace.

Smiles forced, a facade to never decrease,
Eyes holding tears she struggles to confide,
Her spirit trapped in darkness, seeking release.

Loneliness her constant, haunting crease,
Silent screams within her, unheard, unkind,
In the depths of sorrow, she finds no peace.

Invisible chains, her soul they fleece,
Tangled thoughts, a labyrinth to unwind,
Her spirit trapped in darkness, seeking release.

Yet, in her eyes, a flicker of increase,
A glimmer of hope, a chance to remind,
In the depths of sorrow, she finds no peace,
Her spirit trapped in darkness, seeking release.

BRUISE

In the darkest corner of her heart,
    she carried a bruise.
It was a deep, purplish ache that
    murmured of repressed memories,
    forgotten pain.
Each beat of her heart sent
    ripples of sorrow through her veins,
    slight disturbances echoing the
    life she left behind,
    the abuse endured.
She tried to hide her bruised heart,
    painting a smile on her lips
    to deceive the world.
When the moon rose high,
    she would sit by her window,
    allow the bruise to bloom,
    to spread its tendrils across her face,
    like a spider's web of melancholy.
In the solitude of night, she healed,
    one tear at a time.

DAUGHTER'S LAMENT

My mother died today
And the world
Put on a shroud
Of thick dark
Clouds and keened
As the heavens
Opened and rain
Poured heavy and
Cold for a summer day.

My mother died today
And as we gathered
Around her deathbed
We held our own
Wake of remembrance
As we laughed
Through tears
Telling our own: do you
Remember the time when...

My mother died today
And I sat in her room
Surrounded by things
She held dear like
Her favorite book
The spine cracked from
Multiple readings
Each item a recollection
A placeholder for her fragments.

My mother died today
And my thoughts scattered
Like wind-blown ashes
Hers were the hands that
Wiped away tears
Her voice touching me
As only the first voice
You ever hear could
Her smile shining out from her eyes.

My mother died today
And I feel her essence already
In the memories I share
Stories I tell
The love and kindness
I pass unto my daughter
I honor the examples she left
Living as good and full a life
Knowing she will always be.

GOODBYE TO LOVE

Once my dreams gleamed with hope,
    Then, promises shattered, suffocated in deceit;
    The pain of betrayal, a sharp blade in my heart,
    Tears marked my face, as belief and loyalty faded.
I offered my heart, a precious and sincere gift,
    But you callously discarded it;
    In your dishonesty, my world darkened,
    The ache of your betrayal lingered.
Oh, love, once tender, now tainted by deception,
    Moments once cherished now clouded with sorrow;
    I grieved for lost possibilities,
    My shattered heart yearned for comfort.
Well, it's a new day! Goodbye love, I cannot bear your lies,
Yeah, I'm alone, but I am better and stronger without you.

H(A)UNTED

The phantom stalks
In my mind's deep recesses
A twisted reflection of halcyon days
From the depths of my subconscious

I am hunted by a ghostly specter
A former classmate and love once full of life
Who met a tragic end in a crash
His body nearly rent

Nights are cruelest when darkness
Descends like a suffocating shroud
I sense his presence in the wind as
It seeps in around my window's edges

My heart pounds as I catch glimpses
His vacant eyes his still cruel smile
Hear echoes of his voice beseeching release
From eternal torment—a plea for mercy

We once shared dreams and laughter he said
Why did you live while I am dead
You should be here with me he whined
I will snatch your soul he proclaimed

I try to flee but his words reverberate
In my head escape eludes me
His distorted image reflects in mirrors
So I cover them my soul filled with tears

He is determined for me to succumb
But I clutch a faded photograph of him
A captured fragment of time vibrant alive
Not the phantom that stalks my mind

That photograph now almost in tatters
My touchstone to keep him at bay
My heart heavy my reward for surviving
Until it breaks until he steals my spirit

And now in this moment in time
I lie on the coverlet my eyes weary resigned
I hear his cruel laugh feel his breath near
And the photograph crumbles

He holds my spirit close to his
Embracing me preventing my ascent
I look at his ghoulish face see his cruel smile
You've got me I whisper *I am here awhile*

HOPELESS

Shouting with frenzied
Anger at all nothingness;
Echoes of everyday living that
Will not be denied with
A pacing of life's treads,
Ringing with fury in my
Head filled with madness.
Gone, gone all gone to the
Devil and the Flying Dutchman,
Who only receive the lost
And disillusioned into their
Dark world, where the only light
Is the vehemently glowing coals
Flipped, whirring through space
To keep them alive and well done.

SNOWSTORM

We went for a walk
In a driving snowstorm
The wind flung handfuls of
Ice and snow at our faces

And caught
Our breaths
Unaware

You took my hand

I held on tightly—
Afraid to let you go
Afraid my love would not be enough
Afraid the wind would carry you away

I held on tightly—
Until we could breathe freely
Until our love wound healed
Until we were together again

THE GIFT

Once upon
A desolate shore,
A rocky shore,
Where tide pools
Held tiny crabs and
Other small creatures,
He came across
A recently hatched sea turtle,
Its weary form
Attesting to the unforgiving tides.

With a tender,
Reassuring touch,
He cupped his hands
Beneath its tiny body,
Felt its struggle
To survive
Borne by an instinct,
Deeply ingrained.

He lifted it up and away
From its watery prison,
Placing it gently on the sand.
It stilled for a few moments
As if listening to the
Unrelenting waves.
Then, in two or three steps
It caught a wave,
Disappearing into the
Foam-flecked ocean.

Two beings saved
On that desolate shore,
That rocky shore.
As he cupped his hands
Beneath the turtle's body,
It was then...
Yes, at that moment,
It was then he decided
Against walking into the
Ocean's beckoning maw.
It was then he decided
To live.

VIOLET CIRCLES

Your tears lie shimmering,
Pure ice crystals cut from
A heart with no hope glimmering;
The glimmer, the shimmer casting
Bright light, highlighting the
Violet bracelets that are lingering;
Shimmering, shivering,
That everlasting bracelet that
Moves from your arm to your
Heart.

> And your train whistles through your head;
> Carrying your dreams to far-away towns;
> Lofting planes, roaring with the dead;
> Bringing the battered, bruised with the clowns.

Shouting shrill, no cooing doves;
Vulgarities biting, cutting gashes
Through the walls, paper-thin loves,
Slashing, bashing, forever dashing
Hopes you know you must not have;
Those callused hands that are tightening;
Frightening, slicing
Through violet necklaces that
Move from your neck to your
Heart.

> And your train whistles through your head;
> Carrying your dreams to far-away towns;

Lofting planes, roaring with the dead;
Bringing the battered, bruised with the clowns.

WOMAN RISING

In the land of love, where hearts beat as one,
A lover, once true, committed a sin.
The woman stood, her trust and faith undone,
Her heart betrayed; he had let darkness in.

With tears in her eyes, she looked to the skies,
For she had loved him with all her might,
As she cried out in anguish with sorrowful cries,
Now her world was shrouded in darkest night.

Her heart, once filled with love and trust,
Wondered how she could have been so blind,
As shattered, broken, and covered in dust,
She now saw the deceit he had enshrined.

But she refused to be defeated by this blow;
She would rise from the ashes, stronger than before,
For she was a combatant with strength to bestow,
Her heart would not be broken, not anymore.

With fire in her eyes, she faced the truth,
She would walk away with her head held high.
Yes, her love had been tainted by a heart uncouth,
But she deserved a love, pure and true, to abide.

Her spirit unbroken, she would seek a new dawn,
And though betrayed, she would not falter.
Her heart still beat; self-love was not gone;
She was a life soldier, a warrior, a fighter.

Herein lies a lesson to all who love and trust:
Our hearts, though broken, can be mended once more,
Even in betrayal, we must not be crushed;
Our love will shine brighter than it ever did before.

CONTEMPLATIONS

DEEP DELICIOUS BRUSHING

At the end of a day,
With my wild curls untamed,
Mother diligently toiled,
Unraveling each tangled knot.

Once the chaos sat untangled,
Before plaiting my locks into one,
Mother rhythmically brushed the strands,
Creating a harmonious symphony.

Lifting my curls off my nape,
Running her fingers then the brush,
Lifting, smoothing, brushing,
A musical piece all its own.

The gentle pressure of the brush
Against my scalp, a tender massage,
Soothing away the burdens I carried;
A deep, delicious caress of comfort.

As she brushed my hair,
I surrendered to her touch,
The rhythm and gentleness,
Guiding me to a tranquil place.

Closing my eyes, I felt the weight
Of the day lift from my shoulders;
Occasionally, drowsiness overtook,
As I succumbed to her loving care.

Years passed, and the ritual returned,
As I held the brush in my hands,
Repaying the love she bestowed,
Gently brushing her thinning, gray hair.

Each brush stroke, one of love,
Caressing her scalp with tender bristles,
Knowing it brought her comfort,
As she closed her weary eyes.

In those quiet moments,
Our bond grew stronger,
Transcending the limits of time,
A language of love, unspoken yet felt.

I cherish those tender times,
The deep, delicious brushing of
My mother's hair, finding solace,
In my memories and enduring love.

WRITER DREAMING

When shadows dance with whispered secrets,
In the quiet embrace of the night,
I drift into the realm of dreams,
a canvas of infinite possibilities.

Amidst the velvet darkness, a symphony unfolds,
as letters, like celestial beings, emerge from the void;
each shimmering with a soft, otherworldly glow,
their essence, a dance of light and shadow.

They hover, weightless and untethered,
forming a delicate tapestry of language,
twisting and turning in a mesmerizing ballet,
a choreography of the written word.

Words materialize, ethereal and alluring,
hanging in the air like ripe fruit waiting to be plucked,
each one a portal to a world unseen,
a whisper of a story yet to be told.

I reach out, fingertips brushing against
the intangible veil that separates reality from dream,
captivated by the dance of the floating letters,
their movements a language of their own.

In this dreamscape of endless possibilities,
I become a voyager of the mind,
soaring through imagination's maze,
guided by the ethereal glow of the alphabet.

Each letter, each word, a breadcrumb leading
deeper into the tangle of creativity,
where stories bloom like wildflowers in spring,
nourished by the fertile soil of my soul.

And as dawn tiptoes on the horizon,
I awaken, heart heavy with the memory
of the dreamlike ballet of floating letters,
ready to capture their essence in poetic beats.

INCARNATE

Pulsating rhythmic I

Create visions and
Dream...

Of warm, wet sand
Digging, burrowing
With a belly full;
Of rusty clouds at sunset
The wispy, whispering air
Streaming off my wings;

Of fear, as the creamy
Moon stirs the hair at my
Nape, I anticipating
The hunt with the rustling
Leaves deadening my footfalls
Awakening my sense;

Of duty and honor
Glory bent with the cold
Steel pressing into my flesh,
Engraving its form
As the muffled sounds of
Groans surround me;

As a tightening band
Presses against me,
Squeezes me as I ooze
Forward relentlessly;

Full-blown, full-bodied sound
Startles me;

I want more visions
To dream…

Instead, I open my eyes,
Take a breath,
Cry out and
She smiles at me.

KNOCK ON WOOD

In the depths of despair,
    When the walls closed in,
    And homelessness beckoned me,
    Did I utter it in sorrow's embrace?
When love turned to dust,
    And my heart lay shattered,
    With a child in my arms,
    Did I whisper it through tears?
When my friend ventured afar,
    To distant lands
    And foreign shores,
    Did I murmur it, longing for his safe return?
And when he returned,
    And love bloomed
    Like a vibrant flower,
    Did I breathe it with joy?

A thousand times and more
        I say, "knock on wood,"
          Then do it,
            To ward off misfortune,
       Summon fortune's favor.

(I even follow the trend of using my knuckles to rap on my
head)

Yes, a touch of superstition, finding solace
In the ancient belief of
Beseeching the spirits of sacred trees,
To guard against the forces of darkness.

Now, envision it as a prayer,
A call to the benevolent divine,
As I knock on the gates,
To awaken the blessings of heaven.

LISTEN

When the whole house
Has settled into taking the soft,
Gentle breaths of repose,
In the dead of night,
I have lain awake and listened.

It has become a mediation of sorts, this listening.
Everything recedes into the soft,
Dark blurriness of night, and I can
Hear myself, my blood coursing, my muscles
Releasing their hold on the day,
My thoughts being put in order.
I listen and feel.

A certain loneliness is attached to my act of
Meditation because it is, by necessity,
Done in solitude, a solitary practice in which
My secret self obliterates my public self and
The multi-act plays I perform for the world.
It is in that space—with my body stilled,
My heartbeats slowed—that I listen.

I listen to recognize terror so that I can release it
And not have to relive it in my dreams.
I listen to recognize beauty so that I can
Grab it with both hands and hold it close.

In the end, like a miracle, I am recreated.

WRITER, LION, COMB

I find redemption every day
said the writer—
    as she crafted narratives,
    gave voice to complex characters—
by weaving my characters' stories with my own,
healing my old wounds.

I found redemption
said the lion—
    mouth open in a yawn,
    golden mane shimmering in the sun—
by becoming a guardian of the wild,
protecting the fragile balance of nature.

I seek redemption,
said the old comb—
    as it lay forgotten
    on the chest of drawers—
by bringing order to chaos,
restoring confidence and beauty.

MOTE

This morning
    The sun
        Streamed, poured

In through
    My window
        Almost like

Something alive
    And liquid
        And golden

With motes
    Of dust
        Flying, startled

Swimming on
    The beams
        Being transported

My eyes
    Suddenly watering
        An eyelash

I thought
    But no
        Eyelashes were

Lost amongst
    The tears

Making tracks

My cheeks
    Wet, remembering
        Her voice

Explaining words
    Like mote
        "Small particles

Of dust,"
    She said
        As my

Small hands
    Tried capturing
        The fairies

That danced
    And shimmered
        Glimmered, glowed

PROPHECY

We choose our joys and sorrows long before we experience them. —Khalil Gibran

this morning I picked up
my copy of *the prophet*
and thought to myself
we are all prophets

of our own lives
we all make choices
that preordain our lives
we choose our path

through life
what if I hadn't
fallen for my ex-husband
I would have forestalled

heartache peculiar to me
but I would not have
experienced incredible
peculiar heart love that

came with a daughter
who loves as deeply
and makes her own choices
and suffers her own heartache

that preordain her life
then I think about how

life cycles continue
through generations

what if our choices
are also preordained
which begs the question
what about free will?

YEARNING

I yearn for another identity as I gaze upon the stars, planets, and galaxies with their mystic lights in the depths of night.

Oh, how I yearn to be the wind, dancing through the trees, whispering secrets to the leaves. To be weightless, untethered, and free. For the wind knows not the burden of the human heart, carries no regrets, no sorrow. It effortlessly moves through the world, journeying over mountains and valleys, unaffected by duties or desires. It is unencumbered by the intricacies of the human experience, floating effortlessly in the domain of pure existence.

Or perhaps I dream of being a bird, soaring high above the earth. To feel the rush of air beneath my wings, defying gravity's hold. See the world from above, and appreciate the beauty in every landscape, every city, every soul. The bird knows no boundaries, no limitations. It is the embodiment of freedom, effortlessly gliding through the boundless sky.

Maybe I yearn to become a tree deeply rooted in the earth. To stand tall and steadfast, weathering life's tempests. To feel the gentle caress of the sun's rays upon my leaves, nourishing me with warmth. The tree knows the art of patience, of growth, and of resilience—a silent witness, embracing life's cycles with grace.

In truth, it is not the wind, the bird, or the tree I desire to become. It is the essence of what they represent: the freedom, the boundlessness, the rootedness. Being someone or something else allows me to surpass my limitations, transcend my boundaries—a yearning for deeper connections, a longing to experience life differently.

Yet, as I gaze up at the night sky, I am reminded of the beauty that lies within the confines of my skin. It is my humanity that allows me to appreciate the wonder and complexity of this beautiful world.

So, I embrace the desire to be someone or something else but also cherish the unique essence that is inherently mine. Existence weaves together threads, beings, in an interconnected symphony. In this delicate dance, I find comfort, knowing I am part of something greater.

NOTE

Section quotes:

Love & War (page 13)
"You cannot find peace by avoiding life."—Virginia Woolf

Nature & Cosmos (page 45)
"Look deep into nature, and then you will understand everything better."—Albert Einstein

Time & Memories (page 79)
"Time is a game played beautifully by children."—Heraclitus

Seasons & Liminal Spaces (page 111)
"Autumn is a second spring when every leaf is a flower."—Albert Camus

Observations & Views (page 143)
"The world is full of magical things patiently waiting for our wits to grow sharper."—Bertrand Russell

Wounds & Contemplations (page 189)
"The wound is the place where the light gets in."—Rumi

At the beginning of the poem, Prophecy (page 229)

"We choose our joys and sorrows long before we experience them." —Khalil Gibran

ACKNOWLEDGMENTS

I want to thank the editors of *Spillwords*, in which the poetry listed below first appeared:
Battle Scars, Fugue in Blue, Sea Worthy, Violet Circles.

Thank you to Jim Melvin, who included my poem, Transtemporal, in the third book of his Dark Circles series, *Do You Believe in Miracles?*

Acknowledgment is due to the following for their support:

Many thanks to my first readers, Maxine Forrest and Kris Diaz, for their generosity of spirit, time, and dedication.

Many thanks to the talented Laura Simon for using a photo I took on one of our walks and transforming it into a spectacular cover.

Many thanks to Mahshid Amini for seeing beyond the doubts clouding my vision and believing I had a gift worth sharing.

Many thanks to all who support me by reading my work on my website.

I could not have accomplished this without my husband's love and support. His encouragement means the world to me.

Caro Henry, a Caribbean American, has a natural bond with the rhythmic soul of the Caribbean. The soulful beats of the islands, along with the harmonious tunes of reggae music and the colorful tapestry of the native patois of Jamaica and the Cayman Islands, influenced her upbringing. Caro's passion for poetry and storytelling flourished as she grew up in tight-knit Jamaican and Cayman Island communities that cherished them. As Caro adjusted from her Caribbean upbringing to life in America, she found solace in writing, using poetry and short stories to bridge the gap between her past and present.

Caro lives in a Maryland suburb of Washington, DC, with her husband and dog. Besides writing, she tends to her garden and creates a welcoming environment for all the critters (domesticated and wild) that call her yard home. Through her website (https://www.caroehenry.com), she distributes her poetry and stories to the world.